Harri

Harrison

Jonathan Betts

ROYAL
OBSERVATORY
GREENWICH

NATIONAL
MARITIME
MUSEUM

First published in 1993 by the National Maritime Museum.
New, enlarged and revised edition published 2007.

National Maritime Museum
Greenwich
London
SE10 9NF

www.nmm.ac.uk/publishing

ISBN: 978-0-948065-81-1

1

A CIP catalogue record for the book is available from the British Library.

Project management by Abigail Ratcliffe
Drawings by David Penney © copyright
Picture research by Sara Ayad
Production management by Geoff Barlow
Design by Bernard Higton
Origination by XY Digital Limited
Printed and bound in Italy on FSC certified paper by Printer Trento Srl

Mixed Sources
Product group from well-managed
forests, and recycled wood or fibre
www.fsc.org Cert no. CQ-COC-000012
© 1996 Forest Stewardship Council
FSC

Frontispiece: Detail of Harrison's first timekeeper, H1, made in 1730–35 [D6783-1]

Contents

Preface

*T*his little book tells the story of John Harrison (1693–1776), perhaps history's most famous watch and clockmaker. Since Dava Sobel's best-seller *Longitude* was first published in 1995, Harrison has become much better known, but one thing is still missing: a simple and accessible description of Harrison's creations, set alongside the story of his life. Harrison's marine timekeepers and pendulum clocks solved the greatest scientific problem of the age – how to find longitude at sea – and it is in these extraordinary machines that his real achievement lies.

The story of how the timekeepers were made is also a great tale of triumph over adversity: in spite of much prejudice from his peers and many practical and technical difficulties, Harrison's work proved to be one of the major technological achievements of the 18th century. Indeed, his invention, a truly accurate portable timekeeper, was not just the first practical *marine chronometer* but also the foundation of all subsequent precision watches.

A superficial look at his clocks suggests incredibly complex mechanisms, impossible for any but professionals to understand. Many visitors to the Royal Observatory tell us that in fact they admire them primarily as works of art: they are such strikingly beautiful things to see running that they are mainly appreciated as kinetic sculpture. They may be complex to look at, but actually their function is very simple and easy to understand: their sole purpose was to tell the time as accurately as possible. They do not strike the hours, chime the quarters or play music, nor do they have an alarm to wake you up in the morning, as many contemporary clocks and watches did. They do not have complicated calendar indications, automata mechanisms or astronomical indications to amuse, impress and educate.

They do have lots of parts, it is true; and it is also true that those parts were designed and created by Harrison in ways that were unique to him. Being wholly self-taught, and working almost entirely alone, his scientific

John Harrison, painted in oils by Thomas King, *c.*1767. Harrison is shown holding the Jefferys watch and with H3 behind his right shoulder.

and horological thinking was deeply unconventional, and this is one of the most interesting and challenging aspects of studying his mechanisms and writings. Harrison was also a pioneer in his field; it could be said that his was the first government-sponsored research and development project so, by definition, many of his mechanisms and concepts are unique.

Since the 1970s, a small group of independent specialists has been studying Harrison closely, and between us we have made considerable strides forward in our understanding of the man and his work. But there is still much we do not understand and many secrets await disclosure. All that has been said of Harrison to date therefore, including what is in this book, must be regarded as 'the story so far', and very much 'work in progress'.

It is said that imitation is the sincerest form of flattery, and since the 1970s there have been a number of replicas made of Harrison's timekeepers and pendulum clocks. Although cared for by the National Maritime Museum, the marine timekeepers H1 to H4 are the property of the Government, and the official policy of the Ministry of Defence's Hydrographic Department was always to discourage replicas, on the grounds that poor copies would demean the originals. In recent years, however, some very fine replicas have been made by independent craftsmen, even without access to the originals. Currently three full-size and one half-size copy of H1 are known, a copy of H2 and one of H3 were completed in recent years and copies of H4 and the Royal Astronomical Society regulator are believed to be underway. There is no doubt that a great deal can be learned from such projects and, particularly with the replica of H4, it will be fascinating to hear how well they perform.

Acknowledgements

Principal among our little band of Harrison researchers has been Martin Burgess, whose never-flagging enthusiasm, along with his own Harrison-inspired clocks, have been an inspiration to us all. In researching Harrison's life, and particularly his wooden pendulum clocks, Andrew King has contributed enormously to our knowledge. Andrew has also read through the text of this book and has made many very helpful comments and corrections, for which I am exceedingly grateful. Sincere thanks to David Penney for allowing us to use his beautiful drawings, and to the NMM photo studio and publishing teams for seeing this book through to completion. Thanks are also due to Charlotte Henwood and Simon Bird of the Ministry of Defence Art Collection, the current owners of the Harrison marine timekeepers, for permission to continue research on these delicate and historically important artefacts.

John Harrison & Son
A.D 1769

A Brief Introduction to Clockwork

*J*ohn Harrison was a pioneer in the field of precision clockmaking, but he was by no means the first to make mechanical clocks. By the time he was starting his first timepiece, mechanical clocks had been around for over 400 years; there is evidence that clockwork was being made in the late 13th century in Europe. The first examples appear to have been large mechanisms, made in monasteries, as a means of automatically sounding bells for prayer (the term clock derives from the Latin for bell, 'clocca'); made without dials, they sounded the time rather than showing it.

By the beginning of the 14th century, clocks with dials to show the time began to appear in communities across central Europe, as a convenient alternative to the sundial. They were especially useful in cloudy weather but particularly for timekeeping during the night. Of relatively crude construction, made almost entirely of iron and wood, and powered by a weight, these early machines were, however, very poor timekeepers. At the end of a day they might be out by as much as half an hour, and during the first 350 years that clockwork was being made, a sundial was far more trustworthy than a clock. At the time, this did not matter much, as there was usually only one clock in any given community and, right or wrong, at least everyone agreed what time it was!

Left: The movement of H4. The beautifully engraved back of the movement covers the 'high-tech' balance and compensation. The signature records the additional contribution of Harrison's son William. (NMM, on loan from MoD Art Collection) [F7024-008]

11

These diagrams show the insides of a clock. The mechanism is generally known as the **movement**.

The **frame** holds all the working parts of the timekeeper together; in most clocks and watches this is made in brass, consisting of a pair of **plates**, held apart by **pillars**.

At the bottom end of the movement is the power source which is the element that drives the clock, usually a **weight** suspended on a cord or a coiled **mainspring**,

The **wheels** in the movement, which feed the energy to the timekeeping element and supply the correct motion to the hands and dial of the clock, are known as the **train**. Most of the wheels consist of an axle, the **arbor**, with a large toothed wheel and a smaller toothed **pinion** mounted on it. The arbors of the train have at each end a little extension called a **pivot** which, in conventional clocks, runs in a **pivot-hole** in the frame of the clock.

Finally there are the all-important duo, the **escapement** and **controller**, grand-

pinion

arbor

controller

wheel

pivot

weight

Simple medieval iron clock showing the basic elements of a clock mechanism: Driving Force (weight or spring); Train of Wheels (wheel, pinion, arbor, pivot); Escapement (in this example, verge); Controller (in this example foliot, but later could be balance or pendulum).

Verge escapement with a balance, as fitted to clocks and watches.

balance

escapement

escapement

Anchor escapement and long pendulum, as fitted to later longcase clocks.

pendulum suspension

pallets

escape wheel

upper part of long pendulum

sounding names for the most important elements which make up the 'beating heart' of the movement, the part that actually keeps the time. The controller in early clocks was a simple, horizontal bar called a **foliot**, which swung to and fro at the speed determined by the force from the wheels of the clock. Later the foliot was replaced with a simple wheel called a **balance**, and later still, the **pendulum** was introduced as a much more accurate form of controller. The escapement is the part which feeds in the energy to keep the controller swinging, whether it is pendulum or balance. Common longcase clocks in Harrison's day used an **anchor escapement**, so-called because the **pallets**, the parts which receive the push from the wheels of the clock, look like an inverted anchor.

barrel cap

Mainspring and fusee, for equalizing the driving force of the spring.

mainspring

winding square

fusee

barrel   chain or cord

great wheel

verge staff with pallets

escape wheel

pendulum rod

Verge escapement and short pendulum, as fitted to early pendulum clocks.

pendulum bob

With spring-driven clocks, because the spring delivers a force which is much greater when wound up than when it is wound down, from the earliest period of clockwork, spring-driven movements were almost always fitted with a **fusee**. This is a conical pulley (a bit like a tiny fairground 'helter-skelter' with a cord wrapped round it), which ensures a uniform driving force to the wheels of the clock. The mainspring is fitted into a drum (the barrel), around which is a cord which then wraps around the conical fusee. The fusee has the first wheel in the train attached to its base. When the clock is fully wound, and the spring is pulling at its greatest force, the cord pulls on the smallest radius of the fusee; but as the clock runs, and the fusee slowly rotates, so the cord pulls on a greater and greater radius, giving an increasing leverage, at the same time as the mainspring's force diminishes. If matched correctly, the fusee can completely equalize the pull of the mainspring.

By the late 14th century, smaller versions of the large mechanical clocks appeared, made for domestic use, some as alarm clocks only running overnight, and some for timekeeping and striking all day. Then, around 1450 or soon after, there appeared the concept of a coiled spring (instead of a weight hanging on a cord) for driving a clock. For the first time clocks didn't need to be fixed high up on a wall, and could be carried about.

By 1500, during the early Renaissance, cities in southern Germany such as Nuremburg and Augsburg had established themselves as world-renowned centres for fine metalwork, and it was here that clockwork began to be made so small that it could be carried on the person: watches had arrived. Although very expensive to produce, these fine articles of jewellery still kept time no better than before. They were chiefly bought by the wealthy as tokens of prosperity and status, and particularly as symbols of learning and temperance. All this was to change in the following century, as Europe saw an increasingly rational, free-thinking view of science, and the theoretical and practical experiments which now took place would completely revolutionize horological technology.

The first Royal Observatory building, designed by Sir Christopher Wren in 1675 and known today as Flamsteed House. Engraving by Francis Place, *c.*1676. [7228]

A Scientific Golden Age

*T*hroughout the second half of the 17th century, England too enjoyed this scientific 'Golden Age'. Under King Charles II's patronage, the Royal Society was founded in London in 1660 and, with his funding, the Royal Observatory was built at Greenwich in 1675. The works of scientists and mathematicians such as Isaac Newton (1642–1727), Robert Boyle (1627–91) and Robert Hooke (1635–1703) in England reflected a period of intense scientific advancement across northern Europe.

Inspired by the celebrated Italian astronomer Galileo Galilei's (1564–1642) brilliant realization that a swinging pendulum would make a

FACIES SPECULÆ SEPTEN:

highly accurate controller for a timekeeper, the great Dutch scientist Christiaan Huygens (1629–95) designed the first practical pendulum clock in 1656. Whilst the timekeeping of earlier clocks had been in error by about 20 to 30 minutes a day, the new pendulum-controlled clocks were capable of a variation of less than a minute a day: the introduction of the pendulum to clockwork was one of the greatest improvements in the history of timekeeping. The reason the pendulum is such a good timekeeper is that, unlike the controllers in earlier clocks (the foliot or simple balance wheel), the pendulum has a natural 'restoring force' – gravity – which ensures it swings at a very regular rate.

Clockmakers in Holland and France began producing these technological wonders, but it was London clockmakers, most notably Ahasuerus Fromanteel (1607–93), who had sent his son John to Holland to learn of Huygens's invention, who exploited the new design to its maximum potential. In 1675 a similar invention occurred in watchwork – the application of the balance spring. From this time watches too became more accurate (see panel opposite). With the work of these pioneers and the next generation, including the great Thomas Tompion (1639–1713), 'the father of English watchmaking', there began a horological 'Golden Age' to complement the scientific one in England.

By the end of the 17th century, London was universally recognized as the world's most important centre for the manufacture of clocks and watches. Virtually all the important design improvements which shaped the modern mechanical clock were incorporated in English clocks by 1700. Only one real challenge remained to be met in improving clockwork, and it was no wonder the world looked to England for a solution.

THE BALANCE SPRING

Soon after the invention of the pendulum for clockwork, a similar improvement was introduced for watches. Up until then the timekeeping element in watches had been a simple small balance wheel, a tiny version of the kind found in clockwork, swinging to and fro, only controlled by the force from the mainspring of the watch. Now, just as the new pendulum clocks had gravity to control their oscillations more consistently, watches had a little coiled spiral spring applied to the balance, giving its swings a natural frequency too. The principle of applying a spring to the watch balance was first conceived by the great English scientist Robert Hooke in the 1660s, Hooke describing the effect as like applying an 'artificial gravity' to the oscillator. But it was only the spiral form of the spring which was the first really workable design, and this was created by Christiaan Huygens about 1675. Now watches could keep time to about a minute a day, a huge improvement, reminiscent of that in pendulum clocks, and one which led to them sometimes being referred to as 'pendulum watches'.

Balance fitted with a balance spring, in use from 1675.

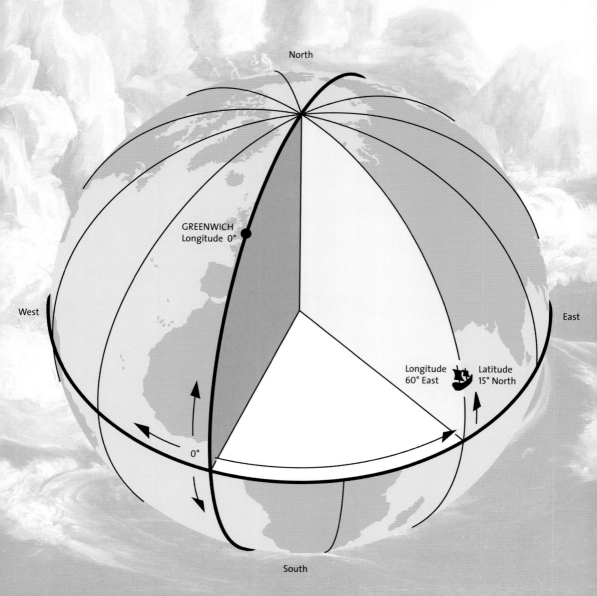

North

West

East

GREENWICH
Longitude 0°

0°

Longitude
60° East

Latitude
15° North

South

The Longitude Problem

From the end of the 15th century, merchants, explorers and adventurers took to the open seas in unprecedented numbers. These journeys were hazardous not only because of the inherent dangers of the sea but also because, once out of sight of land, sailors had no accurate means of knowing their exact position.

One's position on earth is defined by two co-ordinates: *latitude*, one's distance north or south of the Equator; and *longitude*, one's distance east or west from an agreed place, such as one's home port – in other words how far *around* the world one is from home. Latitude was easy to find, with a little calculation, by observation of the Sun at midday or (in the northern hemisphere) by the Pole Star at night. Longitude, however, had always been a problem.

Background: *Wreck of the Amsterdam* attributed to Cornelis Claesz van Wieringen (1580–1633). [BHC0724]

Left: Lines of latitude and longitude on the globe.

Because the Earth revolves on its axis, the Sun appears to traverse the sky from east to west. One complete revolution of the Earth takes one day (24 hours) and we are familiar with the fact that today the world is divided up into twenty-four 'time zones'. In the same way, the circle of the globe can be divided into 360° of longitude so, as the 24 hours of time is the same thing as 360° of longitude, each of the 24 hours is equivalent to 15° of longitude.

Represented by lines known as *meridians* – running from pole to pole, dividing the Earth into these equal segments – longitude is thus the same thing as *time difference* between places. For example, when one calls New York from Greenwich, and it happens to be 12 noon here, we know that at that same moment it will be only 7 a.m. in New York. Therefore, the time difference of 5 hours means that New York is 75° of longitude away from Greenwich.

Longitude is time difference

So, to find your longitude at sea, you need to know, at that moment, what time it is at some other known location on Earth (usually your home port). Then, by noting your local time (which is relatively easy to do, using the Sun or the stars) the difference between the two times provides you with the longitude from home.

The real problem was *how* to discover what time it was at the home port. The obvious answer would be to take a portable clock with you which was set to 'home time' before you left. Such a clock must never be allowed to stop, and would have to be both very accurate *and* unaffected by the violent movements of the ship and temperature changes. In 1700, almost no one believed such a clock could be made.

Having designed the highly successful and practical pendulum clock, Christiaan Huygens made considerable efforts in the 17th century to develop a sea-going clock, as did his great English contemporary Robert

Hooke and a number of other hopefuls. But any marine clock design which relies on gravity for its timekeeping is bound to fail owing to the widely varying forces on board a moving ship, and pendulum clocks could not possibly function reliably under those conditions. Even the great scientist Sir Isaac Newton considered the mechanical clock solution most unlikely to succeed.

A 'celestial' clock

One alternative to the 'impossible clock' was to use the movement of the Moon in the sky as a kind of 'clock' to provide 'home time'. Since its passage past the stars was very predictable, one could use the Moon like the clock's 'hand' with the stars as the clock's 'dial'. By consulting tables listing the position of the Moon at different 'home times', one could calculate one's longitude when at sea. Unfortunately, though, this system – called the lunar-distance method – was complex and time-consuming. It could take four hours to find your longitude this way, besides which, for 20% of the month, the Moon could not easily be seen. Nevertheless, most people believed that the *lunar-distance* method would be the answer to the longitude problem. Indeed, the Royal Observatory was founded at Greenwich in 1675 for the express navigational purpose of making charts of the skies and to record the position of the Moon throughout the year, 'so as to find the so-much-desired longitude of places for perfecting the art of navigation', as the Observatory's Charter states.

The Great Longitude Prize

*M*eanwhile, seafaring nations continued to sail the oceans in spite of the longitude problem, and many lives and huge quantities of cargo were still being lost every year. As early as 1567 the Spanish Crown had offered monetary reward for a solution to this seemingly intractable problem and, in the following century, further prizes were offered by the governments of Portugal, Venice and Holland. The King of France himself had tentatively agreed to reward one particular inventor, who proposed a solution, but it was eventually deemed to be unsatisfactory, and the whole question of determining longitude at sea was considered an impossible task.

The year 1707 witnessed the calamitous loss of the British flagship *Association*, with three other warships, wrecked on the Isles of Scilly, just off the south-west coast of England. The Admiral of the Fleet, the splendidly named Sir Cloudesley Shovell (1650–1707), lost his life, along with nearly 2000 of his men, a disaster as shocking in its day as the loss of the *Titanic* in 1912. Although this terrible accident had not been principally caused by an inability to determine longitude (the fleet were in fact much further *north* than they had estimated), it served as a dramatic and awful reminder of the need for safer navigation at sea, and undoubtedly partly inspired the developments which followed.

In July 1713, the noted mathematicians William Whiston (1667–1752) and Humphrey Ditton (1675–1715) published a letter in the London-based journal, *The Guardian*, stating that they had a solution to the longitude problem and would disclose it if a reward were granted, subject to the inspection and approval of Sir Isaac Newton. The method itself, which proposed 'fixed' barges, 'moored' at regular intervals across the Atlantic Ocean, and from which 'rocket' time signals would be fired, was not practical, to say the least! Nevertheless, Whiston and Ditton were good publicists, as well as friends of Newton's, and the proposal gave the issue of longitude a much higher profile. Pressure was now mounting from

Background: The Admiral of the Fleet, Sir Cloudesley Shovell, and nearly 2000 men lost their lives when four navy ships were wrecked off the Isles of Scilly on 22 October 1707. [1034]

influential merchants, ships'
captains and commanders alike,
for a solution to be found, and
the following year the Government responded by passing an Act of
Parliament offering large prizes for a solution to the longitude problem.

£10,000 was on offer for a solution which could determine longitude to
within one degree, and £15,000 for one within two thirds of a degree.

The greatest prize was £20,000 (equivalent to about £2,000,000 today)
and to win this, the solution – any method would be considered as long as
it was practical – had to provide longitude to within half a degree. To test
the method it would be tried on a ship, sailing 'over the Ocean, from
Great Britain to any such Port in the West Indies, as those Commissioners,
or the major part of them, shall Choose […] without losing their
Longitude beyond the limits before mentioned'. The final somewhat vague
requirement was that the method should prove to be 'tried and found
Practicable and Useful at Sea'.

The impossible question

One unfortunate result of the Act was that the offer of such a huge sum of money attracted the attention of all manner of cranks and charlatans. The official body set up to judge the submissions and administer the rewards, titled 'The Board of Longitude' and made up of senior politicians, high-ranking naval personnel and 'Oxbridge' professors, was flooded with weird and wonderful suggestions. Whiston and Ditton's proposal must have seemed perfectly sane by comparison! The whole longitude question was soon so famous for its difficulty that, like squaring the circle and inventing a perpetual-motion machine, it became a kind of catch-phrase for the pursuits of fools and lunatics. Many simply believed the problem could not be solved and, over the years, commentators often descended to ridicule and heavy sarcasm when referring to the subject.

The 'longitude lunatics' in Bethlem Hospital, from 'The Rake's Progress' by William Hogarth, 1735. One lunatic by the wall attempts to solve the longitude problem by drawing while another looks at the stars through a paper 'telescope'.

Perhaps the most famous example of this was the publication by an anonymous author in 1688 – decades before the Act of Parliament – of a proposal using the 'Powder of Sympathy'. This substance was the brainchild of Sir Kenelm Digby (1603–65), who claimed that patients who had suffered wounds caused by knife or sword were cured simply by placing a bandage from the wound in the mysterious powder. Digby stated that when this was done, the patient immediately felt the effect on the wound, even though they were sometimes a long distance away. The anonymous author of the spoof longitude proposal suggested that every ship be provided with a dog, suitably 'wounded', and at appropriate times back at home, a bandage or knife associated with that wound be plunged into the powder of sympathy, causing the dog to jump, and providing a kind of canine time signal across the miles! It was of course a joke, but to many, the idea that a clock might succeed where dogs had failed was equally ridiculous.

Marine Timekeepers

*I*n spite of the evidence of Christiaan Huygens's failed experiments with a marine timekeeper, there were still a few brave attempts to succeed with a mechanical clock design, especially once the new incentive of the British prize was announced. Until his death in 1727, Isaac Newton was requested to advise on submissions to the Board of Longitude, sent to him via the Admiralty. There is evidence that a number of applications were made, and small sums of money were provided for experiments in the early years, long before the Board of Longitude itself

An early attempt at a marine timekeeper by Henry Sully (1680–1728), 1724. This is 'clock C', one of three known clocks of this type. All failed because they relied on gravity to control the timekeeping. [E8943]

first formally met.

In his correspondence, Newton refers once to a clock design by 'The Quaker'. It is not known for certain who this is, but it is possibly a reference to the well-known Quaker clockmaker Daniel Quare (c.1649–1724), who is believed to have experimented with marine clock designs. Among many published proposals for solving the longitude problem was one by the clockmaker Jeremy Thacker (originally from Beverley in North Yorkshire) who produced a pamphlet, in London in 1714, containing many extremely interesting ideas for a marine clock. However, if such a clock was ever made it does not appear to have succeeded, as nothing more is heard of it.

Determined efforts were also made by Henry Sully (1680–1728), an English clockmaker who worked for most of his life in France. An admirer and follower of Huygens's work, Sully made several attempts during the early 1720s to develop a workable mechanical design, producing and testing three prototype marine clocks. Sadly, all these experiments failed and only served to confirm the widely held view, both in the scientific establishment and among the clockmaking fraternity, that a practical marine timekeeper was simply impossible.

It is remarkable then that not only was a solution to the longitude problem found, but that it should prove to be a timekeeper after all. And what makes the story even more extraordinary is the nature of the man who made this technological breakthrough.

Above and right: Engravings from Sully's published description of his marine timekeeper design. Clock C is shown above. [F7026-1 and F7026-2]

Planche premiere.

Fig. 3.e   Fig. 2.e

B

30 20 10 0 10 20 30
40   G   40
50   50
60   60
70   70
80   80

A   K   L   C

P

Nouvelle
PENDULE
à *Levier*
approuvée par
l'Academie
ROYALE
des Sciences
1724.

I   H

m.1   S   m.2

S

Figure   *premiere*

S

z

z z

T

E   D

HENRICUS SULLY *Londinensis invenit 1723 et fecit 1724.*

à *Paris* — *Gravé par de Rochefort graveur et désignateur du Roy pour l'Academie Royale des Sciences 1728.*

John Harrison, Clockmaker and Scientist

*J*ohn Harrison, a joiner from Lincolnshire, of a relatively humble background and with little formal education, took on the scientific and academic establishment of the day and by sheer determination, coupled with an extraordinary innate technical insight, finally succeeded, winning the Longitude Prize and worldwide acclaim.

Left: Detail from portrait of John Harrison by Thomas King, *c.*1767, showing the Jefferys watch.

Right: Harrison's fourth marine timekeeper, H4, made 1755–59 and considered by many to be the most important watch ever constructed. [F7024-001]

Childhood and Education

*B*orn on 24 March 1693 at Foulby, near Wakefield in Yorkshire, John Harrison was the eldest son of Henry Harrison, an estate carpenter, believed to have been employed by Sir Rowland Winn at Nostell Priory, next to Foulby. When John was about four years old, the family moved to the remote village of Barrow in neighbouring Lincolnshire, on the south bank of the Humber, just south of the large and rapidly expanding port of Hull. Here the Harrisons were established as notable members of the local community, with John's father soon taking up the role of Parish clerk. They had four further children: two girls, Mary and Elizabeth, and two boys, Henry and James.

Little is known of John's early education, but this is likely to have been acquired at home, along with the woodworking skills taught him by his father. Harrison was, nevertheless, a precocious youth, sufficiently bright to catch the attention of a visiting clergyman who, when John was a young man, lent him a copy of the celebrated lectures on mechanics by Nicolas Saunderson (1682–1739), Lucasian Professor of Mathematics at Cambridge. Harrison copied out the whole book. It remained a treasured possession and over the years he annotated it with copious notes. John also learned the art of land surveying, making his own plane table and compass, the portable instrument used in the field by surveyors at that period for making maps.

Harrison also displayed a great interest in music during his childhood – an interest both theoretical and practical, which was to stay with him throughout his life. He became an accomplished bass-viol player and was the choirmaster at the Barrow parish church. He also retuned the bells at Holy Trinity and St Mary Lowgate churches in Hull. In later life, Harrison published a radically different method for tuning the musical scale. He even understood that the high-frequency oscillations of musical instruments have implications for timekeeping design.

This map of the Humber, dated 1734, shows both Hull and Barrow, at a time when Harrison was constructing and testing H1.

Clockmaking Begins

*W*here Harrison's interest in clockmaking came from, we simply do not know. We do know that in 1713, at the age of twenty, he had completed a longcase clock which, while relatively ordinary in external appearance, has a mechanism made almost entirely of wood. Although this choice of material may seem logical enough for one trained as a joiner, making small clock mechanisms out of wood was unheard of in England. There were a few continental precedents emanating from Southern Germany and one or two characteristics of Harrison's early work suggest the influence of continental clockwork, so it is possible that he came across examples of these in the port of Hull.

Three of Harrison's early wooden clocks have survived. The first, with the movement signed and dated 1713, is now preserved in the Worshipful Company of Clockmakers' Collection, in the Guildhall, London. The second, similarly signed, and dated 1715, is now in the Science Museum, London. The third, dated 1717, is at Nostell Priory, though acquired in the early 20th century and not directly as a result of Harrison's origins there.

The movement of Harrison's earliest surviving longcase clock, dating from 1713. Although made of oak and boxwood, the design is otherwise similar to ordinary clocks of the day. [D6769]

The Early Clocks

*S*imply constructed in oak, these clocks all have the conventional anchor escapement and the countwheel system of hour-striking, standard for longcase clocks at the time. The wheels and pinions are also made of wood, the wheels of oak and the pinions of boxwood (*Buxus sempervirens*). Even in these early clocks, Harrison's ingenuity is seen. In constructing his wheels, he used the mill-wright's technique of morticing segments of three or four teeth into the rim. This enabled him to cut the segments along the grain of the wood which, by inserting them radially into the wheel, made the teeth considerably stronger. Having said this, in other respects the clocks are basically wooden versions of contemporary metal clock designs and, with steel pivots and brass bushes in the wooden frame, these movements still required oiling in the usual way.

Today, none of these clocks has its original case, but a section of the trunk door of the 1717 clock does exist in the Clockmakers' Company Collection. It provides an interesting insight into Harrison's education. Pasted to this piece of the door is a manuscript giving times of sunrise and sunset throughout the year, and an equation table. This table provides data, for each day of the year, showing the difference between 'mean time' (uniform, clock time), and 'solar time' (time by a sundial, which varies throughout the year). An equation table thus enables one to set clocks correctly using a sundial. The table is in Harrison's own hand and suggests he may have had sufficient astronomical knowledge to determine the data himself.

In 1718 John had married but, tragically, his wife Elizabeth died just eight years later. Within six months, Harrison had married again, to another Elizabeth. During the latter part of his early career as a clockmaker, John had his younger brother, James (1704–66), to help him and it seems that the two developed an interest in the technical aspects of clocks and watches. For example, the brothers began to time pocket watches in several different positions to study the effects of gravity on their time-keeping, a very early example of what became standard

The 'Equation of Time' table, pasted to the inside door of Harrison's pendulum clock of 1717. This enabled the owner to set the clock using a sundial.

practice in precision watchmaking in the 19th and 20th centuries. Perhaps these experiments were associated with Harrison's early interest in winning the Longitude Prize, though Harrison states that he did not hear of this until 1726.

The Brocklesby Park Clock

*T*he Harrison brothers' first major clockmaking project – and an important early commission for them – was a revolutionary turret clock made in the early 1720s for the stables at Brocklesby Park, the seat of the Pelham family (later the Earls Yarborough). The clock, which was also constructed almost entirely of oak, was revolutionary because it needed no lubrication. Even modern clock oil tends to thicken with age,

The movement of the clock in the stables at Brocklesby Park, Lincolnshire, made by the Harrison brothers c.1722. This revolutionary clock proved to be the foundation stone for John Harrison's later precision clock designs.

to creep away from where it is needed and to turn acidic or evaporate. Mostly deriving from animal fats, 18th-century oils were particularly poor and tended to be one of the major causes of clocks failing to work.

With no formal education, John Harrison was always a radical thinker. Instead of worrying about ways to improve the oil, he designed a clock that didn't need it, the first of its kind and one of only a few ever to have been made. Harrison was particularly adept at selecting the best materials for an application and again employed boxwood, this time for the bearings in the clock, which, in combination with brass pivots, provided a very effective oil-free bearing surface. Later, he discovered that the dense, greasy, tropical hardwood lignum vitae (*Guaiacum officinale*), again in combination with brass, would perform even better in this application.

The clock originally had an anchor escapement, but Harrison soon improved this with a new invention, the grasshopper escapement, which employed no sliding actions and, therefore, did not require oiling. The escapement was given this peculiar name because of the action of its pallets (the two little pieces which receive the pushes or impulses from the clock mechanism). To avoid sliding actions, which would need lubricating, these pallets, which were made of oak, are designed to 'jump' out of engagement after each impulse, their action being reminiscent of the hind legs of a grasshopper.

As well as being exceptionally well designed, the Brocklesby Park clock is exceptionally beautifully made, revealing Harrison's first-rate skills as a joiner and cabinet maker. Over 280 years after its construction, the clock is still at Brocklesby Park, continuing to run reliably and keep excellent time – and still without the need for lubrication.

The oak wheelwork, with lignum vitae roller pinions, and the grasshopper escapement of Harrison's precision pendulum clocks.

The Precision Pendulum Clocks

*F*lushed with this success, Harrison continued to develop more accurate and reliable clock designs. In the mid-1720s, under his direction, James Harrison set to work on a series of remarkable precision pendulum clocks – smaller, longcase versions of the turret clock – to see just how far they could push the capabilities of this design. Superficially these clocks look like Harrison's early longcase clocks, but in detail they are very different indeed. Like the turret clock, they run without lubrication, having smaller versions of his grasshopper escapement and using lignum vitae bearings. The wheelwork is still of oak, but now the pinions are made of little lignum vitae rollers, mounted on brass pins, so the wheel teeth are actually in rolling contact during meshing. Three of these precision longcase clocks have survived, being dated 1726, 1727 and 1728, the latter on display in the Clockmakers' Company Museum in London.

John Harrison's victory over the problem of lubrication by eliminating the problem itself was ingenious, but not typical of his scientific method. His usual approach was to accept the presence of an 'enemy' and negate the effect by compensating for it. Using this more typical method, he eliminated another significant error in these precision pendulum clocks: that caused by the effects of temperature change.

The cottage on Barton Road, Barrow to which Harrison moved in 1726. Sadly it was demolished in 1968 while being considered for listed building status.

Left: Harrison's first precision pendulum clock, made in 1726. This clock was one of a pair Harrison used as his time standard, and also as test-beds for his precision clock development.

Right: The 'gridiron' temperature-compensated pendulum designed by John Harrison in 1726, which contributed to the clocks' incredible accuracy of a variation of no more than a second in a month. Fine adjustments were made to the compensation using the 'tin-whistle' adjuster (shown).

Temperature Compensation

*C*locks go slower when they get warmer because the pendulum rod expands and lengthens, and longer pendulums beat more slowly than shorter ones. For it to keep time constantly, the pendulum's *effective length* must not change. The effective length is the distance between the point of suspension and the centre of gravity. Harrison solved the problem of temperature change by inventing a pendulum which, instead of a simple rod, has a gridiron made up of an alternating series of brass and steel rods, the steel rods' downward expansion being counteracted by the upward expansion of the brass rods. In this brilliantly clever design, although all the rods are expanding, the effective length of the pendulum remains the same and it continues to keep time.

As a result, Harrison tells us that these early precision pendulum clocks achieved the astonishing accuracy of a variation of no greater than 1 second in a month, a performance far exceeding the best London clocks of the day. And because the clocks had no oil, they maintained their performance for much longer than conventional clocks. Harrison developed two of these clocks in his workshop in tandem, his ingenious scientific method being to use one of the clocks as a control while he made adjustments and improvements to the other, then switching the clocks and using the improved clock as a control while the other was adjusted. Both these clocks were then employed as regulators, to test his other clocks. He tells us that, in order to time them precisely, he used the passage of stars across the sky at night (see right). This highly ingenious method was suggested in Saunderson's lectures, Harrison doubtless learning of it from his copy of these. Using this method, Harrison was able to gauge time to the remarkable precision of a twentieth of a second.

Harrison's time standard: accurate time was derived by observing the exact moment particular stars disappeared, when aligned with the glazing bars of his window and a neighbour's chimney.

The Marine Timekeepers

A simple calculation based on the terms of the Longitude Act tells us that, in order to qualify for the main longitude prize of £20,000, a timekeeper would have to keep time with a variation no greater than 2.8 seconds a day. Before 1750, the only commonly available portable timepieces, watches, were hopelessly inaccurate; even the very highest-quality watches of that period lost or gained at least a minute a day. The only timepieces capable of the required accuracy were large pendulum clocks, fixed rigidly to the wall like Harrison's regulators. So, given the options available to them, potential designers of marine timekeepers, such as Harrison, saw only one logical course of action: to win the longitude prize, they would have to make a portable version of a precision pendulum clock. As we shall see, however, this progressive and apparently logical approach was not the correct one, but no one realized this at the time.

In the following few years, Harrison therefore formulated a plan for a large marine timekeeper, and it is recorded (some years later, just after Harrison's death) that he visited London in about 1727 or 1728, to seek support to make it. Harrison himself certainly tells us that he came south at about this time to seek funding and moral support, taking with him drawings and a written description of his proposal for the timekeeper.

It has been suggested by Harrison's biographer, Humphrey Quill (1897–1987), that this visit was more likely to have been two or three years

Harrison's signature at the end of the 1730 manuscript. This document summarised Harrison's proposals for his first marine timekeeper, H1. [D6770]

*p John Harrison, Clock=
Maker at Barrow; Near
Barton upon Humber;
Lincolnshire.*

Astronomer Royal, Edmond Halley, by Sir Godfrey Kneller, *c.*1720. Halley encouraged Harrison and recommended he consult George Graham. [BHC2734]

Left: The great watchmaker George Graham, by Thomas Hudson, *c.*1740. Graham gave Harrison advice and moral support, as well as some money to get him started in making H1.

later, in 1730, as a manuscript description of his first marine timekeeper, dated that year, has survived. ('The 1730 manuscript', as this little book is known, is now preserved in the Clockmakers' Company Collection). However, it is just as likely that Harrison did come to London in 1727 or 1728 with preliminary sketches, and that the 1730 manuscript, which is very carefully worded and illustrated, is a refined version, the result of further development and advice – possibly intended for use on a follow-up visit to London.

Whichever year the first visit was, Harrison records that he went initially to Greenwich to seek the advice of the Astronomer Royal. At the time, this was Edmond Halley (*c.*1656–1742), of comet fame, who received Harrison very kindly (Halley was at the time, according to Harrison, despairing of ever completing the 'lunar tables' containing the data required for the lunar distance method). Halley, however, not being in any way horologically qualified, felt unable to judge the soundness of the plans, and suggested that Harrison go directly up to London to see George Graham (*c.*1674–1751). Graham had been partner to Thomas Tompion, and was, at the time, the greatest and most highly respected maker of watches, clocks and instruments. Halley therefore warned Harrison to be brief and to the point; it is clear that Harrison was not the best at expressing himself succinctly, and what with making his clocks from wood, and being based in the wilds of Lincolnshire, one can understand that someone as busy and important as Graham may have initially been prejudiced in his assessment of who he was dealing with. Harrison writes of Halley:

[He] caution'd me how to begin with Mr Graham [...] in as few words as possible to let him to understand that I had indeed something worthy [of] notice to communicate to him; but as notwithstanding that piece of advice

and my doing my best [...] Mr Graham began, as I thought it very roughly with me [...] which [...] occasion'd me to become rough too; but however, we got the ice broke [...] and indeed, he became as at last, vastly surpris'd at the Thoughts or Methods I had taken. Harrison, having arrived at 10 a.m., was still discussing timekeeper design with Graham at dinner in Graham's house late into the evening. Graham even extended the offer of a loan to support Harrison's work: a greater demonstration of confidence could not be imagined. It is interesting to speculate at what point the 'ice broke' in their discussion, and which particular 'thoughts or methods' impressed the great watchmaker. It is known that, since at least 1715, Graham himself had been trying to design a pendulum with temperature compensation using brass and steel rods, but he had not been able to work out how to do it; in the end he came up with another system, using mercury in a glass jar as the bob of the pendulum. No doubt when Harrison showed him how he had designed his type of compensation pendulum, Graham realized this was no ordinary carpenter from the country.

On returning to Barrow, Harrison spent the next five years or so, with his brother James, constructing the extraordinary timekeeper known today as 'H1'. After preliminary but rigorous tests on a barge on the River Humber, Harrison felt ready to have the machine tested more formally. H1 was brought to Graham in London and publicly displayed to the scientific community. It became quite a celebrity, hugely impressing all who inspected it, and was widely regarded as one of the wonders of the age. Harrison was besieged with requests to see the timekeeper by both scientists and socialites. It is also possible that some came to see Harrison the man: the curiosity from the country, the ingenious clockmaker.

In 1735, the Royal Society (whose members included Graham and Halley) issued a certificate of H1's great potential, which was then used to persuade the authorities to grant the new timekeeper some form of trial. Up until his death eight years before, Newton had been asked to consider the viability of all such proposals, but now it fell to the Admiralty's other advisers to recommend to the First Lord of the Admiralty that Harrison and his timekeeper should be given a semi-official trial. And so it was that H1 and its maker sailed, on board the warship *Centurion*, to Lisbon in May 1736.

Before departing, the ship's captain, George Proctor (d.1736), wrote that he found Harrison 'a very sober, very industrious and withal, a very modest man' but he feared that at sea 'the difficulty of measuring time truly [...] gives me concern for the honest man and makes me fear he has attempted impossibilities'. After a week-long voyage in tempestuous weather, Proctor wrote from Lisbon that Harrison 'was sea sick withal, but [...] seems satisfied that the motion of the ship was not in the least detrimental to its keeping true time'. The ship's log however reveals H1 not performing as well as it might on the outward voyage, and some of the positions calculated from its readings appear to be considerably wide of the mark. In Lisbon, H1 was transferred to the *Orford*, and does appear to have performed much better on the long homeward voyage. Indeed, Harrison used H1 to correct a misreading of the ship's longitude and prevented what could have been a very serious incident. All the officers believed that the first land sighted by the ship was 'The Start' (Start Point near Dartmouth). Harrison and H1, however, proved that it was 'The Lizard' (Lizard Point on the Penzance Peninsula). This is located nearly sixty miles to the south-west – it is the southernmost point in England – and revealed to the crew that the ship was in fact in a much more perilous position, enabling evasive action to be taken in the nick of time. In due course, in recognition of this significant feat, the Master of the ship, Roger Wills, presented Harrison with a certificate outlining these important facts.

On 30 June 1737, the Board of Longitude was convened officially, for the first time, to hear how H1's trial had gone and to inspect this model of 'high technology'. The news the Board received was evidence that, after all, a marine timekeeper might just prove to be a practical solution to the

'H1', the First Workable Marine Timekeeper

*T*oday, 'timekeepers' are referred to as marine chronometers, but the term chronometer was not widely used until after Harrison's death. The word 'timekeeper', however, had very special significance; it was only used to describe a portable machine capable of high accuracy. It should also be mentioned that the 'H' abbreviations, used today to refer to the timekeepers, are a relatively recent denomination, first applied by Lieutenant-Commander Rupert T. Gould in the 1940s during his restoration work on them.

As mentioned, Harrison designed his first marine timekeeper to be, conceptually, a 'portable' version of his precision pendulum clocks, and it is important to bear this in mind if one is to understand H1 properly. Unlike the pendulum clocks, which go for a week with one winding, all Harrison's timekeepers run for one day only, but H1 has wheelwork of oak with lignum vitae roller pinions. The main frame and ancillaries of the timekeeper are all made in brass or other alloys, where possible avoiding the use of steel which would rust at sea. Instead, Harrison used two types of bronze, a low-tin bronze where good tensile strength was required, and a high-tin bronze where high compression strength was needed. The major difference between H1 and the pendulum clocks is that H1 does not require gravity for any of its operations – an essential prerequisite for a marine timekeeper, but one which many earlier designers, including Huygens and Sully, had overlooked. Thus the timekeeper is spring-driven, with a fusee to ensure a uniform driving force. This fusee is however most unusual in that it employs two chains and two barrels, positioned at 180° to one another, hugely reducing the load on the pivots of the fusee.

In spite of its relatively good performance on the *Orford*, H1 did not perform nearly well enough to win even the smallest of the longitude prizes. Even before its trial Harrison probably knew the design could be improved; it was after all very much a prototype, and one on which the Harrisons never even put their signatures. Wishing to move on, Harrison didn't ask for a second, official trial of H1, but requested financial assistance from the

Harrison's first marine timekeeper, H1, made in 1730–35. The dials, clockwise from the top, are for seconds, hours, calendar and minutes.
(NMM, on loan from MoD Art Collection) [D6783-3]

Incorporated within the fusee of H1 is one of Harrison's inventions which would prove of lasting benefit to chronometer- and watchmakers. This was his form of the mechanism known as *maintaining power*. In weight-driven clocks, and in spring-driven clocks with a fusee, when one winds the mechanism up, the drive to the wheels is temporarily removed and the clock may lose time, or even stop working. To get round this, the mechanism is fitted with maintaining power, which ensures a continuing drive during winding. The pre-Harrison version of this mechanism had to be actuated manually, but Harrison's type is automatic and one is unaware of its operation during winding. By the late 18th century virtually all precision clocks, watches and chronometers employed this device.

The movement of H1 is considerably larger than the wooden longcase clock movements, weighing 34 kg and standing 63 cm high. For the timekeeping element, Harrison replaced the pendulum with two interlinked bar-balances (like a pair of dumbbells, see right), connected across their centres with cross–ribbons – a type of frictionless gearing – between them. The balances swing in anti-phase (i.e. towards and away from each other) and the interconnection between them was supposed to ensure that any motion affecting one balance was largely counteracted by that same effect on the other balance. It is true that if the machine is turned around while running it does appear 'not to notice' that it is

H1's balances are linked at the centre with 'cross-over' ribbons. Harrison believed they would be unaffected by external motions.

being moved. The balances are also linked with helical steel springs at top and bottom, to provide a restoring force, like gravity acting on a pendulum (like Hooke before him, Harrison referred to these springs as providing his 'artificial gravity'). So, when swung apart, the balances oscillate together, each swing taking 1 second.

The balances themselves do not run directly in the frame of the clock, but sit and roll, on special 'anti-friction' segments (see below), to render their action almost frictionless. Thus, with an adapted version of the grasshopper escapement and the other elaborate anti-friction devices kept in the design, the clock required no lubrication. Harrison also adapted the gridiron

principle from his pendulum in order to compensate for changes in temperature. In balance-controlled timekeepers, a rise in temperature not only causes the balance to get larger, which will make it swing slower, but a higher temperature will also cause the balance springs to become weaker, reducing the 'artificial gravity' and making the slowing effect even greater.

An important technical point about H1's temperature compensation was that, just as in his pendulum clocks, Harrison realized that to perform at its best, the compensating mechanism should be built into the balances themselves, and they were originally constructed that way. Unfortunately he was unable to design a system which worked reliably, and was forced to rearrange the gridirons in a fixed position within the frame of the clock. Nevertheless, in later years he still maintained that the compensation would be best within the balance, and in the years after his death the principle of a compensation balance was accepted as the norm for all precision watches and chronometers.

Each of H1's balances rolls between two small segments of wheels and, because there is no sliding action, no oiling is required.

Board to make an improved version of the timekeeper. Nothing like H1 had ever been seen before and the Commissioners were undoubtedly very impressed both by the machine and by its inventor. They allocated him £250 there and then, with the promise of another £250 on completion of an approved machine. In agreeing to this support, the Commissioners were, in effect, instigating the very first government-sponsored research and development project undertaken by a private contractor.

The Move to London

On his visits to London, and especially once he had been introduced to George Graham's circle, Harrison discovered how the city's unique horological facilities and connections made work easier. Almost anything he needed in the way of horological services or materials could be sourced in London. There is no doubt either that Graham and his circle would have been able to advise Harrison on written scientific and horological sources (though there were few of the latter in English at the time), and we know Graham himself discussed and advised Harrison on some details of his timekeepers (advice that was not always taken).

Harrison now decided that if he were to succeed in creating a marine timekeeper, he would need the support of the London trade, and he moved to the capital in 1736, soon after his return from Lisbon. His first home was in Leather Lane, in Holborn, but in about 1739 he moved west to Red Lion Square, where he would remain for the rest of his life. It seems that James accompanied his brother for the first year or so, but there may have been a breakdown in the partnership as James did not stay long; by 1738 he was certainly living back in Lincolnshire.

The Second Timekeeper, 'H2'

*H*arrison began work on the second timekeeper immediately and, by January 1741, he was before the Board again. By this time he had already realized a deficiency in the design of H2 and had begun work on a third timekeeper, H3. Notwithstanding this, H2 is as remarkable a timekeeper as H1 and has a more professional feel to its construction. Harrison told the Board in a later interview that he had employed the services of a number of London tradesmen; this would certainly have been for the supply of materials such as brass plate and steel springs, and services such as engraving. In all probability he also employed workmen for tasks such as basic finishing, although the main design and layout of the movement would have been all his own, the details of which would have been carefully concealed from prying eyes.

Larger and heavier that H1, H2 stands 66 cm high, weighs over 39 kg and is made almost entirely of brass. The only wood in the timekeeper is in the lignum vitae parts and the oak pallets of the escapement. The concept is fundamentally the same as H1's, except that the temperature compensation is of a simplified design and Harrison fitted a remontoir to H2.

As with H1, H2 would originally have been cased and mounted in large gimbals to ensure it remained horizontal at all times. The mounting itself

THE REMONTOIR

In an ordinary clock, which has a long series of wheels to supply power to the escapement, small errors in manufacture of the wheels cause variations in the driving force. This, in turn, causes variation in timekeeping. The remontoir is intended to remove these variations. A small spring directly drives the escapement, independently of the main wheel train. The function of the main train was now simply to wind up this small spring at regular intervals, as and when it needed it. In H2, this rewinding occurs every 3 minutes 45 seconds.

does not survive but its form has been recorded in a small pen-and-ink colourwash sketch by John Charnock (1756–1807), drawn at Greenwich about 1780 and showing H2 in its complete state.

Harrison recorded that he noted a deficiency in the linked bar balances when H2 was moved. As in H1, the cross-linking of H2's balances was supposed to render them insensible to external motions while running. But he discovered, very much to his consternation, that the timekeeper was somewhat affected by movement, owing to centrifugal force acting on the balances. If subjected to circular motion in a horizontal plane, the timekeeper would tend to go slow; if subjected to circular motion in the plane of the side elevation, the timekeeper would tend to gain; and if subjected to circular motion in the plane of the front elevation, the timekeeping would become unpredictable, tending to gain or lose.

This tiny colourwash drawing of H2 was done by the artist John Charnock, c.1780. It shows the original gimballed mounting, now missing. [PW2941]

He realized that the reason for this, in the first two types of motion, was that the balances were in the form of dumbbells; had he made them in the form of wheels, the problem would be removed. But there was no room in H2's design to convert it to having wheel balances, so after more than two years of hard work and considerable expense, he was obliged to set H2 aside and start again. Any official trial must give him the best possible results: he may not be given another chance and he could not contemplate having H2 tested once he discovered this fault.

Harrison's backers stayed with him, and petitioned the Board on his behalf for more money to continue with H3. Still highly impressed with his ingenuity, the Commissioners duly awarded Harrison another £500, and work continued on the nascent third timekeeper.

H2 took Harrison, with the help of London craftsmen, just two years to make – from 1737 to 1739. It is the heaviest of the timekeepers. (NMM, on loan from MoD Art Collection) [D6784-1]

Harrison's Third Timekeeper, 'H3'

*U*nfortunately for Harrison, H3 was to be even more problematic than H2. Within five years it was running and under test, but from the outset it was clear that getting this design to keep close time would be difficult, and Harrison was obliged to make constant changes to it. Years went by and although many improvements were made, Harrison just could not get this timekeeper to perform to prize-winning accuracy. Even after an astonishing nineteen years of painstaking labour, H3 was stubbornly refusing to keep time well enough, and although he learned a great deal from this herculean endeavour, its ultimate role was solely to convince him that the solution lay in another design altogether. So, after his initial success with H1, the 1740s and early 1750s must have proved something of a mid-life crisis for Harrison.

However, none of this was known to the Board of Longitude, who continued to support him with grants until 1760, awarding him over £3000 during the period. His supporters and other members of the scientific community were also unaware of the great difficulties Harrison faced, and were still pinning their hopes on H3's success. Indeed, aware of the much wider implication for science in what Harrison was attempting, and even though H3 had still not provided the breakthrough, in 1749 the Royal Society awarded Harrison its highest honour, the gold Copley Medal, for his research work.

H3 itself, which was supposed to be Harrison's magnum opus, must have been the greatest technical disappointment of his life. In later years he could only refer to it wryly as 'my curious third machine', and his perplexed notes on this machine represent the only example on record of the great man admitting to failure. Nevertheless, H3 is an extraordinary mechanism and contains inventions which would prove exceedingly important in the history of technology. The timekeeper stands 59 cm high and weighs 27 kg (43 kg in its case). The balances are wheels instead of dumbbells and are arranged one above the other. They are still linked together with cross-wires, beat seconds and are driven by the grasshopper

H3, Harrison's third marine timekeeper, took him nineteen years to construct and adjust (1740–59), though its timekeeping never quite came up to his expectations. (NMM, on loan from MoD Art Collection) [D6785-5]

JOHN HARRISON

THE BIMETALLIC STRIP

In order to compensate for temperature changes in H3, Harrison created a new and revolutionary device, the bimetallic strip. This consisted of two flat strips, one of brass, one of steel, riveted together. Because brass expands more than steel with a rise in temperature, this bimetal bends into a curved shape with the brass on the convex side, and will bend back the other way if the temperature falls. With one end fixed, the movement of the other end of this device can then be used to adjust the

balance spring automatically with changes in temperature. A shorter spring is normally stiffer, so, with a rise in temperature, the bimetal shortens the spring slightly, compensating exactly for the effects of temperature. The bimetallic strip was a tremendously versatile invention and would come into its own in the 20th century. Most households today use the bimetallic strip as a thermostatic control in central heating, electric kettles, irons, toasters and so on.

H3's improved temperature compensation was the bimetallic strip, another of Harrison's brilliant inventions that is still very much in use today.

escapement as with earlier machines. For his 'artificial gravity', instead of helical springs Harrison fitted one short spiral spring, which controls the upper balance only; a 30-second remontoir was fitted to provide uniform power supply; and the machine runs without lubrication as with the previous timekeepers. H3 was mounted like H2, in a glazed brass case, and is depicted behind Harrison in the portrait by Thomas King (d.c.1769) (see page 7).

The Caged Roller Bearing

Another important invention that Harrison created for H3 was the caged roller bearing, the ultimate evolution of his anti-friction devices. The central pivot of the bearing is surrounded by a series of bronze rollers, mounted in a circle, in a little brass cage. These rollers run round inside a circular bronze track. When it is revolving, the pivot can take loading in any direction, and the rollers will support it, in rolling contact. The whole assembly is virtually frictionless and requires no lubrication. In effect, it is the predecessor of the caged ball bearing, a device used in virtually every complex machine made today.

One of the caged roller bearings from H3. This seminal design of Harrison's would, in the 19th century, develop into the caged ball bearing, and was of immense technological importance.

Isochronism

One of the biggest problems Harrison had with H3 was ensuring that the swings of the balances were *isochronous*. This complex-sounding word (pronounced 'I sock ronnus') in fact describes a very simple concept. For a balance or pendulum to be isochronous simply means that all the swings, whether large or small, take the same time. Therefore if the drive to the balances should occasionally be a little reduced, which would make the swings of the balances a little smaller, the timekeeping would still be correct. The balances of H3 however were not isochronous, and Harrison spent many years trying to understand why, and finding ways to correct the problem. In fact the main problem lay in his use of the single, short spiral balance spring. But at this period, the complex science of spiral balance springs, which would be central to the later development of precision watches in the 19th century, was still largely a mystery. It is not surprising, then, that Harrison had such difficulties, but there is no doubt that he learned a great deal about balances and springs from his struggles with H3, so his 19 years were certainly not entirely wasted.

Other Work by Harrison

*W*e know very little about Harrison's other activities during his life in London. Everything seems to have revolved around his work on the timekeepers and it seems highly unlikely that he, or his wife Elizabeth, had much time for socializing at any stage of their lives. We do know that Harrison's interest in music remained as strong as ever and that he continued to advise on the tuning of musical instruments and bells.

He also occasionally took on private horological commissions. For example, in 1755 he designed a new form of anchor escapement for the turret clock at Trinity College Cambridge, for which he was paid three guineas. The escapement was actually made for Trinity by another clockmaker, William Smith of Upper Moorfields (now Finsbury Square) in London. Unfortunately, the clock no longer exists (except for its setting dial), but there are four known surviving examples of Harrison's escapement in other clocks made by Smith, and all still working, in England.

Below, left: The Harrison-type anchor escapement from one of four surviving turret clocks made by William Smith c. 1760.

Below, right: The setting dial from the clock at Trinity College Cambridge. This is all that survives of the first clock with Harrison's anchor escapement of 1755.

Drawing of a new form of anchor escapement, designed by Harrison for the turret clock in Trinity College, Cambridge, in 1755. He was paid three guineas for it.

The R.A.S. Regulator

*I*n parallel with his work on H3, from 1740 Harrison was also busy working on an equivalent regulator, to supersede his wooden-movement precision pendulum clocks, by then nearly 15 years old. This clock, now known as the R.A.S. regulator (the clock belongs to the Royal Astronomical Society) was, as far as we know, never finally adjusted by Harrison. Creating this clock was, in one sense, like the work on H3 in that it involved a long process of design and adjustment. However, in every other sense it was totally unlike H3, because this design was highly successful. So good was the performance Harrison was getting from it that he predicted that one day, once finally adjusted, this regulator would be able to keep time with variations no greater than 1 second in a hundred days. This feat was not achieved until William H. Shortt (1881–1971) introduced his 'free pendulum' clock in the early 1920s, but modern experiments with designs based on Harrison's original have shown that, given time, Harrison could well have proved his claim.

It was developing a successful marine timekeeper which was Harrison's principal concern, however, and by the early 1750s, while continuing his struggles and failures with H3, he was doing what all good inventors do and looking elsewhere at the same time, to see if there wasn't another way to crack this problem.

The R.A.S. (Royal Astronomical Society) regulator. Made by Harrison in parallel with H3, this fixed, pendulum-controlled clock was Harrison's last word in regulator design. He predicted a variation of no more than a second in a hundred days from it. (NMM, on loan from the Royal Astronomical Society) [D6786-1]

The Breakthrough

*A*mong the small number of horologists and scientists who still believed a marine timekeeper was a possibility, very few had seriously contemplated the idea that something on the scale of a pocket watch, as opposed to a large clock, would ever be viable. After all, everyone knew what poor timekeepers watches were; when even the best could only manage about a minute a day, watches weren't even close contenders for the longitude prize.

That is not to say there wasn't interest in improving the performance of watches; there is evidence that, from the late 1740s, serious experiments were being made. In 1752, one noted London watchmaker, John Ellicott (1702/3–72), announced to the Royal Society that, following ideas he developed in 1748 (using bimetallic technology undoubtedly inspired by Harrison's well-known work), he had had a watch fitted with temperature compensation. However, Ellicott stated that before describing it to the Society he would wait and see whether it did indeed improve the watch's timekeeping. Nothing more was heard of this experiment, and it is reasonable to conclude that the watch did not, after all, perform well. This conclusion is confirmed by a remark made by Harrison a few years later, in 1763, after his watch H4 was, to everyone's disbelief, going exceptionally well. He complained: 'but they still say a watch is [...] but a watch, and that Mr Ellicott has tried what a watch will do and that the performance of mine (though nearly to truth itself) must be altogether a deception'.

It is known that from at least the early 1750s Harrison was also experimenting with improvements in watches, although whether he began after hearing of Ellicott's work, or vice versa, we will probably never know; for one who was, at the time, looking for alternative technologies to H3, Harrison may well have been prompted to look again at watches anyway.

The Jefferys Watch

What is certain is that at about the same time, in 1751 or 1752, Harrison commissioned a London watchmaker, John Jefferys, to make him a watch following Harrison's own designs. The watch, which Harrison would have finished and adjusted himself, was evidently intended for experimental use – it might have been useful for his astronomical observing and clock testing, but was undoubtedly intended as a potential prototype marine timekeeper, depending on how well it performed. The watch was given a bimetal for temperature compensation, of course, but it had another feature which was much more significant for its timekeeping properties.

Up until the 1750s, watchmakers had always made the balance in their watches relatively light and small, so they oscillated with relatively low energy. The reason for this was that it was an absolute article of faith among professional watchmakers that, if a watch had run down and stopped, when it was wound up again, it must immediately spring into life, i.e. it must be 'self-starting'. One can imagine them saying, 'What's the use of a watch if you have to shake it to get it started?' The only way they knew to achieve this was by making the balance small and light, so that the

The movement of the Jefferys watch. With its high-energy balance it performed very well and was the breakthrough Harrison needed.

The Jefferys watch. Completed in 1753, this watch was made to Harrison's design by John Jefferys. It is the watch shown in Harrison's hand in his portrait. The discolouration is due to fire damage sustained during the 1940s.

escapement of the watch could easily push the balance to set the mechanism in motion.

Harrison's instincts told him, however, that in order for a watch to keep good time, its balance must oscillate with as much stored energy as possible. But to achieve this meant going completely against that cardinal rule in the watchmaker's book. The balance he designed for the Jefferys watch was relatively heavy (he gave it a rim of gold), was somewhat larger than usual and beat faster than normal watches (the balance beats five times in a second: it has, as watchmakers would say, 'an 18,000 train', i.e. it beats 18,000 times an hour). The watch had a verge escapement – the standard watch escapement of the day – but one that was completely redesigned, enabling the balance to run at a much larger amplitude (i.e. with bigger swings than normal). All of this meant that the watch was by no means self-starting, and, if the watch ran down, the case had to be given a little twist after winding up for it to start running. With this redesign, Harrison had expected a moderate improvement in timekeeping, but to his amazement the improvement was very great indeed, and he began to realize the way forward.

After all this time, he had in fact been working on a false assumption. The huge, slow-swinging oscillators of his pendulum clocks are fine if they are fixed to a very solid foundation, but if one wishes to start moving a timekeeper around, one has to rethink the technology altogether, as the large slow-beating balances are inherently unstable and prone to disturbance. The solution was, after all, in those 'hopeless' little things called watches, but it was vital that the oscillator within them was of the 'high energy' type for them to succeed. This apparently simple discovery is one of Harrison's great achievements.

The minutes of the Board for the meeting held on 18 June 1755 introduce the first hint to the outside world of what Harrison knew to be his breakthrough. As well as asking for money to continue H3, he requests support:

[…] to make two watches, one of such a size as may be worn in the pocket & the other bigger […] having good reason to think from the performance of one already executed according to his direction (i.e. the Jefferys watch) *[…] that such small machines may be rendered capable of being of great service with respect to the Longitude at sea […]*

Support was duly provided by the Board and Harrison began work immediately. Over the next four years he produced the one which was 'bigger', a watch which would in more recent times be known as 'H4', arguably the most important watch ever constructed.

The 'Lesser Watch'

Even today we are not sure whether the smaller watch, the 'one of such a size as may be worn in the pocket', was ever made. The Board certainly awarded Harrison money to make it, and we know he made a construction drawing of the movement, as this survives in the Clockmakers' Company Collection. Harrison also refers to it in his writings, calling it his 'lesser watch' (meaning smaller watch), which suggests it might have been made.

So where is it? Nobody knows. The lesser watch has in recent years become legendary after its fictional 'discovery' in the final episode of the cult BBC sitcom 'Only Fools and Horses' broadcast at Christmas 1996. The main character, 'Del Boy' Trotter, 'sold' the watch through Sotheby's for £6,200,000, making him and his sidekick, Rodney, millionaires. Appropriately enough, the watch was 'purchased' on behalf of the National Maritime Museum at Greenwich, and all were happy ever after! Well, we can always dream.

That last episode was watched by 24.6 million viewers, more than the Queen's Christmas speech and the England vs Germany football match in the World Cup that year! It gave the staff at Greenwich a few headaches afterwards, however: we were flooded with claims to have found the real lesser watch, something which, alas, has not yet come to pass.

Harrison's construction drawing for the movement of the 'lesser watch', c.1755. It is not known if the watch was ever completed.

a b   Note, the distance between the two Lines
a, b, is right in this Draught, but is somewhat
too great in the Draughts to which this belongs:
And it is to be observed that one of the Pillars
must be plac'd a little farther from the end of
the Ballance spring. ~~But it is to be noted,~~
~~see below~~

But it is to be noted, that what
I thought of gaining, as in this
Draught &c. viz, from the Ballance
being transfer'd to the other side of
a Watch I afterwards consider'd
would be nothing, or at least very
immaterial; hence, as in common the
most proper.

Harrison's Fourth Timekeeper, 'H4'

*N*ot surprisingly, then, in most respects the large silver-cased watch that Harrison made next – just 13 cm in diameter and weighing 1.45 kg – is completely different from the earlier marine timekeepers, though the same logical approach to design and the same construction methods are evident.

Both externally and to some extent internally, H4 looks like a very large contemporary pocket watch, even to the extent of having pair cases (with an inner case for the movement and a protective outer case around it). Technically, however, it is different from an ordinary 18th-century watch in a number of significant ways. Apart from being exceptionally finely constructed, the movement's balance is much larger, and of higher frequency. Like the Jefferys watch, H4's balance oscillates five times a second and, having the same escapement, the oscillations are much larger than in an ordinary watch. Temperature change was compensated for in the same way, by using a smaller version of H3's bimetallic strip. Unlike the Jefferys watch, H4 contains a miniature H3-type remontoir, rewinding eight times a minute, to ensure a constant drive to the escapement. Although Harrison was unable to miniaturize his anti-friction devices, and H4 (like the Jefferys watch) required oil on all its bearing surfaces, jewelled bearings were fitted in many places to reduce friction to a minimum. The use of jewelled bearings was not Harrison's invention – they had been in use by London watchmakers since the beginning of the century – but the extent to which he used them was unprecedented, as was his use of diamond in the specially shaped pallets of the escapement. Harrison records that during H4's construction he had great difficulty forming the smooth curves he needed on these pallets (which were his means of ensuring that the balance and spring were isochronous), but he did succeed, and even today, in spite of close study, we are still uncertain how.

The special 'isochronal' verge escapement of H4. It is still uncertain how Harrison formed the curved backs of the diamond pallets (in blue).

The solid silver pair case is interesting. The inner, with the incuse (stamped) mark 'I H', and London hallmarks for 1759/60, might just have been made by Harrison himself. The inner case would have been needed first, to protect the movement during the process of final construction and adjustments and, most importantly, to prevent prying eyes from seeing what was inside. The outer case, hallmarked for London 1760/61, is marked 'H T' and was possibly made by Henry Thompson, a 'small worker' and joiner in Silver Street, close to Harrison's house in Red Lion Square.

Trials and Rewards

*H*arrison had made great progress with H4, but he was now not the only one coming closer to solving the longitude problem. At the very next meeting of the Board of Longitude, in March 1756, the Commissioners were told of some lunar tables recently completed by Professor Tobias Mayer of Göttingen University, which had been produced in parallel with the work of the Royal Observatory. Furthermore, the invention of the reflecting quadrant (the octant) by John Hadley (1682–1744) in 1731 (simultaneously with Thomas Godfrey (1704–49) in Philadelphia) made measuring the altitude of stars at sea much easier and provided the sort of results that could be used in conjunction with the new tables. The then Astronomer Royal himself, James Bradley (1693–1762), recommended that the Board reconsider the potential of the lunar-distance method for solving the longitude problem, as it was now a sufficiently accurate method and was becoming a really viable alternative to timekeepers.

At the Board's meeting on 18 July 1760, Harrison asked for a trial of H3, hoping that it would be possible to send 'the watch' (H4) as well, as it had far exceeded his expectations. He said he needed one more winter to test its temperature compensation, and this was allowed. In March 1761, £250 was allocated to John's son, William Harrison (born in 1728 and now in partnership with his father) so he could prepare for a trial voyage to Jamaica in charge of the timekeepers.

After innumerable delays, on 18 November 1761 the *Deptford* sailed for the West Indies with William and H4 (in the event, H3 was not sent with them). The

Medallion portrait of John Harrison in vitreous enamel, by James Tassie, *c.*1760. [D5577]

Deptford sailed for the West Indies with William and H4 (in the event, H3 was not sent with them). The watch had been set to exact local time at Portsmouth, by careful observation of the Sun at noon (a process known as 'equal altitudes'). As chance would have it, the crew's supply of beer (fresh water did not stay drinkable on long voyages) had become tainted en route, and the ship urgently needed to put in at Madeira for provisions. Using H4, William was able to predict correctly that, at the time, they were nearly a hundred miles closer to land than the navigating officer had judged, an achievement happily noted by the whole crew. Indeed, the Captain, Dudley Digges, was so impressed that he asked to purchase the next example of such a timekeeper Harrison might make.

The voyage on to Jamaica was equally successful for H4. William proved to the ship's company that their longitude was well over a hundred miles different from their reckoning. They arrived at Jamaica on 19 January 1762 (the official end of the trial). After ascertaining exact local time at Port Royal by equal altitudes, it was evident that the watch had gone extremely well, though exactly how well would only be determined after careful calculations on returning home.

The passage back to England could not have been more different from the placid, happy voyage out. With few ships available at the time, William had been obliged to accept a cabin on the small sloop-of-war *Merlin*, and the weather throughout the voyage was tempestuous, to say the least. At times, William had to cradle H4 in blankets to protect it from buffeting and seawater. He insisted, however, on keeping it going lest it should be thought too fragile to stand use at sea. On arrival at Portsmouth its error, according to William's reckoning, was only 1 minute 54.5 seconds after a total period of 147 days. And calculations on the watch's performance during the official trial then showed it to have been in error by just 5.1 seconds during the whole voyage out! Needless to say, the Harrisons were very pleased.

It was a remarkable achievement but, alas, it was spoilt by one crucial oversight. There had been a failure to officially discuss and agree the *rate* of the watch. Even very accurate, reliable timekeepers do not usually keep exact time. It is extremely difficult to adjust a clock or watch so it does not gain or lose anything. As long as the amount is regular and predictable this really doesn't matter. If, for example, it gains 5 seconds each day (its 'rate') then one simply makes that much allowance every day and correct time can be deduced. However, for trials, this concept was entirely new. Since the Harrisons had not officially declared H4's rate before leaving port, there was absolutely no way for Board members to know if it was, indeed, as accurate as William claimed it was. The trial was therefore next to useless.

Predictably, the Board of Longitude were not convinced by William's figures. At their meeting in June 1762, they announced that they were dissatisfied with the trial on a number of counts but, not surprisingly, top of the agenda was the question of applying a rate. In fairness to the

A Sixth Rate on the Stocks by John Cleveley senior, 1758. The painting shows (right) a sixth-rate ship of the line, virtually identical to the *Tartar*, and in the foreground is a sloop-of-war identical to *Merlin*, both ships used for the trials of H4. [BHC1045]

Harrisons, it is clear that the whole trial had been badly organized from the outset, and the Board were equally culpable in the uncertain results. They did however agree to award £2500, of which £1000 was only to be paid after another trial, terms to which the Harrisons reluctantly agreed.

From this point on, the attitude of the Board began to harden towards the Harrisons. The reasons for this are complex and not all the motives are entirely clear even today, but one element which certainly didn't help was that, as the years went by, Harrison's old influential friends were dying (e.g. Graham in 1751 and Bradley in 1762) and he was losing his establishment support. Another problem was the definite prejudice of members of the Board against timekeepers as a solution; many years later one of the Commissioners claimed that the Board had never expected a timekeeper to qualify for an award at all.

Even as late as 1792, Nevil Maskelyne (1732–1811), Astronomer Royal and member of the Board, was still asserting that lunar distances were more trustworthy for fixing longitudes, and it was only in the 1820s that the Royal Navy finally appeared to accept the chronometer as the best means for longitude determination. For many Commissioners, the seeds of doubt must have been sown during the previous 19 years during which, in retrospect, Harrison surely appeared to have been floundering with H3. Now, as the contender suddenly appeared to be a watch, and looking much like an ordinary one, they were even less inclined to believe it could be successful. As quoted earlier, in 1763 Harrison himself complained bitterly about people claiming watches were just watches and could never succeed.

Considerations of character also should not be underestimated. We know, from his writings, that Harrison had difficulty expressing himself clearly. From one point of view, this is hardly surprising. Many of the concepts and devices he was trying to describe had no name and he was constantly having to invent a new technological language. This, taken in combination with his humble origins, his lack of formal education, and his probable lack of social graces must have stood Harrison in poor stead before such an elite as the Board of Longitude, especially as very large sums of money were at stake. After all, the Board had a huge responsibility: they were answerable to Parliament and the nation, and posterity would judge them harshly if they disposed of such a vast sum of money without absolute proof that the winning method would be practical and genuinely solve the problem.

Furthermore, the image of William Harrison that has come down to us from contemporary accounts suggests he was not his father's best ally before the Board. He comes across as a decidedly objectionable character, a nouveau riche socialite of a rather unpleasant kind. It should also be remembered that the Board were constantly changing. Hardly any two meetings of the Commissioners were made up of the same people and, as the years went by, those less supportive of Harrison (and timekeepers) became a majority.

Add to this the emergence of the increasingly perfected lunar tables, a mathematical solution which undoubtedly appealed more to them as theoreticians, and perhaps the diminishing favour accorded the Harrisons is not so difficult to understand. Unfortunately the hardening attitude of the Board was matched by mounting paranoia and suspicion on the Harrisons' side, evidenced by an increasingly argumentative and sullen attitude before the Commissioners.

At the meeting of the Board in August 1762, Harrison confirmed his agreement to a second trial of H4 to the West Indies. Remembering the dangers met during the return from the earlier trial, the Board also persuaded Harrison of the benefits of a formal disclosure of the technical make-up of H4, to which he tentatively agreed.

There must have been a certain breakdown in communication between the Board and Harrison on this matter, however, as it seems the Board's intention was always that details of H4 should be made widely known for the benefit of the international scientific community, whereas the Harrisons evidently understood that what they were passing on was absolutely secret and for British interests only.

Two of Harrison's construction drawings for the movement of H4, *c.*1755

French Interest

The Board of Longitude, believing a disclosure was now imminent, informed representatives from France that a visit to inspect the timekeeper was on the cards. In April 1763 the celebrated French astronomer Jérôme Lalande (1732–1807) visited Harrison and was able to get a look at the external appearance of the watch, but failed to get any details of its interior. Then, in company with the mathematician Charles-Étienne Camus (1699–1768) and clockmaker Ferdinand Berthoud (1727–1807), he duly visited Harrison again in May, but this time the three were only shown the large timekeepers, Harrison stubbornly refusing to let them see H4 at all.

As a way of keeping the pressure on the Board, Harrison petitioned Parliament for a formal clarification of his situation. This 'clarification' took the form of an Act of Parliament, which came into force on 31 March 1763. It guaranteed that no one else could win the prize with a timekeeper until his had been properly tried. The Board, however, then augmented this by applying a set of rather severe requirements for the 'disclosure' of the construction of H4, adding that Harrison should oversee the making of two more watches. These would be tested to ensure that the information had been passed on effectively and to prove that others could satisfactorily make copies of H4.

Harrison refused to accept these extra conditions and there was an impasse. Neither party was willing to agree on a compromise and so the question of the disclosure was shelved while plans were made for the H4's second trial to the West Indies. When the Board met on 4 August 1763 to make the necessary arrangements, the first item on the agenda was the dreaded question of deciding H4's rate. It was finally agreed that Harrison should be allowed to provide his own statement of what rate it should be. The astronomers were then nominated to carry out the necessary observations during the voyage, one being Nevil Maskelyne, an ardent supporter of the lunar-distance method of finding longitude and, not surprisingly, soon to be Harrison's *bête noir*.

Portrait of the fifth Astronomer Royal, Nevil Maskelyne, attributed to John Russell, drawn c.1776 in black and red chalks on blue paper. [75064]

In August 1763, Maskelyne was sent out to Barbados to set up the observation station which, on the arrival of the watch, would enable it to be compared to local time by equal altitudes. Maskelyne was also charged with making other land-based astronomical observations, in order to fix the longitude of the island with greater certainty. On his voyage out, Maskelyne had taken the opportunity to continue his tests of the lunar-distance method of determining longitude and was extremely proud of the accurate results he obtained.

Meanwhile, after making his declaration of H4's rate (gaining 1 second a day in ambient temperature) to the Admiralty on 24 March 1764, William Harrison and Thomas Wyatt, a companion, departed with H4 in the ship *Tartar* from Spithead at Portsmouth on the 28th. As with the earlier trial, William predicted the arrival at Madeira with extraordinary accuracy. Captain Sir John Lindsay presented William with a certificate to that effect and all seemed to be going well, until William's arrival at Barbados.

No sooner had William stepped ashore, than rumours reached his ears that Maskelyne had been boasting about the success of the lunar-distance method he had employed to find longitude on his passage out from England. Understandably, William felt that Maskelyne was not the man to compile an unbiased report on the timekeeper and, after heated discussion, it was decided to appoint one of the other astronomers, Charles Green (1734–71), to share Maskelyne's work.

In the event, the trial was another astonishing success story for H4. The average computation put the watch's error at just 39.2 seconds after the voyage of 47 days.

This was *three times* better than the performance needed to win the £20,000 longitude prize. Whatever may have been said and done before, the Board should now have recognized that the Prize had been won. Sadly, the Board saw matters differently. Remembering the clause in the original Act of Parliament that the method 'should be practicable and useful', they were not yet ready to pay anything. First, they raised the old spectre of the disclosure and stated that they would pay half the total, £10,000, once Harrison had made a proper exposé of H4's mechanism, on oath, to a specially appointed committee. The details would then be published for the benefit of the world at large. Second, the Board implied that the watch was a fluke and that others of the same kind should be made and tested. Third, the Board then had these requirements sanctioned in an Act of Parliament, which also included the demand that all four timekeepers should be handed over once the £10,000 had been paid to Harrison.

At this stage the Harrisons' relations with the Board were at an all-time low. To fuel their paranoia, the man they were learning to distrust above all others, Nevil Maskelyne, had been appointed Astronomer Royal in 1765 and was therefore an ex-officio member of the Board. For several weeks, Harrison refused to negotiate any point of the Board's proposals, but the mood of the Board of Longitude was equally militant. Realizing that they would get nowhere if he didn't compromise, John Harrison finally agreed to sign the oath and disclose the inner workings of the watch.

Anticipating this, the Board had already arranged a panel of six experts to inspect the watch and witness the explanation. The panel consisted of three well-respected practical watchmakers – Thomas Mudge (c.1715–94), William Matthews (dates unknown) and Larcum Kendall (1719–90); the Reverends William Ludlam (c.1717–88) and John Michell (1724–93); and the London instrument maker John Bird (1709–76). Larcum Kendall had been apprenticed to John Jefferys and, as Jefferys had died in 1754, Kendall may well have helped Harrison with the making of some parts of H4.

The disclosure meeting could scarcely have been a relaxed affair under these circumstances, but – to add to the tension – the Board appointed Maskelyne to oversee the presentation. Beginning on Wednesday 14 August 1765, the panel gathered at Harrison's house in Red Lion Square and watched him dismantle H4. They heard Harrison's answers to the technical questions put to him and he also provided drawings of the watch for further explanation. On 22 August, the panel were apparently satisfied, and each member signed a certificate stating that the disclosure had been complete (though later at least one of them expressed doubts as to having learned everything they needed).

The Board met again on 28 October 1765 and granted Harrison enough money to make up £10,000, the first half of the full reward. In return, they insisted on the other stipulation: that the timekeepers should all be handed over to them. After numerous pleas from John they grudgingly allowed him to hold on to H1, H2 and H3. They insisted on having H4 though, as they intended to ask Larcum Kendall to produce a copy of it, to reassure them that workable copies could be made.

At last Harrison had half the prize. But, for him, it was only the whole reward, and the recognition that went with it, that mattered. Since the failed visit in 1763, the French clockmaker Ferdinand Berthoud had, via a third party, remained in contact with Harrison, and now, apparently feeling cheated of his rightful rewards, Harrison agreed to negotiate with the French for details of H4. He received Berthoud in London in early 1766 but, expecting £4000 for his disclosure, he sent him away again on discovering that Berthoud had come with only £500! Not to be put off, Berthoud then approached one of the Board's own disclosure panel, the watchmaker Thomas Mudge.

Unfortunately for Harrison, Mudge, a man of great integrity, was happy to oblige with information, believing it to be the Board's intention that the knowledge should be disseminated. Needless to say, the Harrisons were not happy on discovering what they considered to be a breach of trust and published a broadsheet on the matter. Fortunately for Harrison, Berthoud was not sufficiently talented to make good use of what Mudge had conveyed, and the machines he later made in Paris bear only surface similarities to Harrison's work.

The whole matter was to some extent made irrelevant a year or so later, as in April 1767 the Board published *The Principles of Mr Harrison's Timekeeper*, and this was translated into French within a few weeks. Although at the time this publication was said to have been of insufficient use to those wishing to continue developing marine timekeepers, the evidence today shows that in fact it was immensely influential and was arguably the most seminal of all publications in the history of the chronometer.

The Principles of Mr Harrison's Timekeeper, 1767. Although limited in the information it contained, this book was highly influential in the fundamentals it revealed to the next generation of chronometer makers. [F7025]

THE
PRINCIPLES

OF

MR. HARRISON'S TIME-KEEPER,

WITH

PLATES OF THE SAME.

PUBLISHED BY ORDER OF

THE COMMISSIONERS OF LONGITUDE.

LONDON:

PRINTED BY W. RICHARDSON AND S. CLARK;

AND SOLD BY

JOHN NOURSE, AND MESS. MOUNT AND PAGE.

M. DCC. LXVII.

The Second £10,000

*H*arrison now knew that, in order to qualify for the second part of the Longitude Prize, he had to produce at least two other watches similar to H4 and have them tested. He wrote to the Board suggesting two alternatives: he could make the two himself, for which he would need a grant of £800, or he could set up a factory and employ other workmen to make any number of them under his supervision. The latter proposal was contingent on his being paid the £10,000 in advance.

Unfortunately, Harrison was in no position to bargain with the Board. In their reply of 26 April 1766, the Board flatly refused either proposition, telling *him* to make the two timekeepers (particularly difficult since they had taken H4 from him). They would decide about the reward only after the two timekeepers had been tested. Reading between the lines, it seems that the Board was sending a clear message. In receiving half the reward, they considered Harrison had done well and should not be awarded any more unless he absolutely met the requirements of the new Act.

However, knowing that he would not give up the challenge of winning the whole longitude prize, they decided to test all four timekeepers at Greenwich, a completely pointless exercise as Harrison's claim lay in the performance of H4, not the larger machines. Nevertheless, on 25 May 1766, without any advance warning, Nevil Maskelyne, of all people, turned up at Red Lion Square to collect H1, H2 and H3 from Harrison. To add insult to injury, Maskelyne arrived with an unsprung cart – the sort of transport that could do more damage to Harrison's timekeepers than years at sea! Harrison was extremely reluctant to advise how they should be best moved, lest he be implicated if they were damaged in transit. Predictably, one of the timekeepers (H1) was dropped.

H4 goes on Trial at the Observatory

*I*n the meantime, H4 began its ten-month trial at the Observatory; a trial which, it seems, was destined to go badly from the very outset. Owing to the fact that H4 had not been cleaned or properly readjusted since its dismantling for the disclosure, which Harrison really ought to have ensured, and because it did not have entirely fair treatment while under Maskelyne's care at the Observatory, it did not perform at all well. In the end, both parties must share some responsibility for the poor results of the trial. The conclusions of Maskelyne's published report, however, are not surprising: '[…] Mr Harrison's watch cannot be depended upon to keep the Longitude within a degree in a West India Voyage of Six Weeks […]'.

The fact that Harrison's watch had been dependable on at least one such voyage was completely obscured by the so-called formal trial. Harrison was incensed, immediately publishing a virulent response, *Remarks on a pamphlet lately published*, but to no avail.

Harrison's Fifth Timekeeper, 'H5'

*G*reatly embittered but still determined to see the project to its end, Harrison and his son began to make the first 'copy timekeeper' to qualify for the remaining prize money. On 11 April 1767, Harrison approached the Board, again requesting the loan of H4 so that he could make an accurate copy. The Board refused, saying that Larcum Kendall needed H4 in order to make his copy. They also informed Harrison, to his horror, that they had devised a whole new, ten-month plan for testing the watches.

In spite of this further setback, Harrison (now in his mid-seventies) and his son continued working for over two years on the fifth timekeeper, known today as 'H5'. Meanwhile, Kendall's good progress on his copy of H4 had the adverse effect of persuading the Board that all Harrison's difficulties to date had been merely procrastinations. Kendall's watch, known today as 'K1', was completed in 1769 and was inspected in early 1770 by the same panel that had seen H4. William Harrison was also present at the demonstration and admitted the copy was exceptional. Another request to the Board that both K1 and H5 be considered as the 'two timekeepers' for an official trial was also turned down. The Harrisons were told, in no uncertain terms, that it was they who must make both timekeepers.

By 1772, further finishing and adjusting of H5 had provided only one further timekeeper. The idea that John Harrison himself, now 79, might sit down and make a second watch was clearly absurd. Father and son had reached the end of the road and desperate measures were now needed if further progress was to be made. The Board were obviously no longer prepared to dedicate much more time to the Harrisons; their interests lay elsewhere. With Maskelyne's *Nautical Almanac* now being published every year, and the navigational instrument, the octant, now available in a much-improved form, the sextant, the lunar-distance method had become entirely viable.

It is thus true to say that the members of the Board of Longitude were prejudiced against timekeepers as a viable means of finding longitude. It is

Harrison's fifth timekeeper, H5, completed in 1770. Although much plainer in appearance, the watch was technically very similar to H4, with slightly improved temperature compensation. (Worshipful Company of Clockmakers, inv. 598) [D6768]

not however true that members of the Board engaged in a vendetta against Harrison, nor that they falsified evidence in their favour; they were simply doing what they believed to be right given their huge responsibility, and they just didn't believe timekeepers would ever be a reliable solution.

Besides, even if Harrison's timekeepers did prove themselves useful, they needed to be much less expensive before the Admiralty could afford to equip the fleet. K1 cost the Board £500 – the equivalent of about £25,000 in today's money. The price of just 50 K1s could buy a complete second-rate ship of the line, armed and ready for sea! Harrison's was a very expensive design and thus not considered practicable.

King George III

*S*ensing he had almost run out of options, as a last resort John decided to appeal to the highest authority in the land, the King himself, who Harrison knew had been following his fortunes with interest. An approach was made to George III on 31 January 1772 by letter, via the King's private astronomer at Richmond, Stephen Demainbray (1710–82). William Harrison requested an opportunity for H5 to be put on trial by the King himself at his private observatory. William was summoned for interview at Windsor and asked to expand on some of the details. At this interview the King is said to have remarked: 'these people have been cruelly treated', then exclaiming: 'By God, Harrison, I will see you righted!'

The King was keen to help, and agreed to put H5 on trial at Richmond from May to July of that year as a form of independent test. After a false start, apparently caused by leaving the watch too close to some magnetic lodestones, H5 performed superbly. Its daily rate of variation over the whole 10 weeks averaged out at less than a third of a second per day. Both the King and Demainbray were very impressed and the Harrisons believed their own personal trial was nearing its end.

Hoping that the involvement of the King might cause some change of heart in the Commissioners, Harrison approached the Board of Longitude again on 28 November, citing H5's good behaviour and asking for the remaining £10,000. It was a vain hope. The Board replied that only an official trial would suffice and that 'no regard will be shewn to the result of any trial made of them in any other way'.

Probably at the suggestion of the King himself, Harrison now formally approached the Prime Minister, Lord North, with the full story. This appeal had the interesting effect of causing the Speaker of the House of Commons to instruct the Board of Longitude to reassess the case in William Harrison's presence, witnessed by two MPs who were Harrison supporters. At this meeting, the Commissioners posed a number of specific, formal questions to William who, somewhat churlishly, gave only

Portrait of King George III, by Johann Zoffany, 1771. The King was a great supporter of the Harrisons at the time that members of the Board of Longitude were objecting to awards of prize money to them.

abrupt answers, mostly in the negative. When finally asked why he refused now to submit just one timekeeper to a trial, he replied: 'For the following reasons … Loss of time, Expense attending it, Uncertainty of reward afterwards and I think I can employ my time better.' The Board's minutes continue: 'He then withdrew.' With that, all contact between the Board and the Harrisons ended.

Harrison's petition to Parliament required further redrafting before it could be guaranteed a successful result. Finally, the recommendations of a specially appointed parliamentary Finance Committee were accepted by the House on 21 June 1773. The Act of Parliament entitled 13 George III,

George III's private observatory at Richmond. H5 was tested here between May and July 1772 and performed exceptionally well. From *Kew Gardens: A Series of Twenty-Four Drawings on Stone.* Lithograph by Charles Hullmandel after George Ernest Papendiek, 1820.

chapter 77, duly received Royal Assent and Harrison was awarded £8750. This was not the £10,000 for which Harrison was hoping, but if one adds it to all the sums he had from the Board before, including expenses, the final sum actually totals over £23,000. Harrison had, at last, received the great longitude prize money.

The interesting question remains as to whether Harrison had actually 'won' the full Longitude Prize. The members of the Board of Longitude were opposed to the final payment, and it could be argued that without their approval one cannot say the full prize had been won. It might also be argued, as no doubt Harrison did, that all the sums, excepting the first £10,000 and Parliament's £8750, were not reward but were covering his costs; but it is not clear from the Board's deliberations what was, and was not, considered by them as expenses. However, it was agreed by Act of Parliament that Harrison should receive the money he did, and, whether they liked it or not, that money was all paid to him through the Board of Longitude's own accounts, so it can also be argued that the prize was effectively won.

Perhaps more important to John was that the reward be seen to be his. It still rankled with him that the members of the Board had not approved the granting of the money, but here was some recognition that John Harrison had solved the longitude problem.

Less than three years later, on 24 March 1776, Harrison died at Red Lion Square. It was his 83rd birthday.

Conclusion

*I*n 1772, Larcum Kendall's copy of H4, K1, was given the most exacting trial imaginable when it was issued to Captain James Cook (1728–79) on his second voyage of discovery to the South Seas. It performed magnificently. From his own log of the voyage we can read of Cook's steady conversion towards belief in the timekeeper. From being a traditionalist and one who had learned to trust the lunar-distance method on his first voyage, the second voyage saw Cook gradually won over by using an instrument he had faith in. References such as 'our trusty friend the watch' and 'our never failing guide' speak volumes from a man of Cook's abilities and experience. K1 was used by Cook on both his second and third voyages, to chart many Pacific islands and north-eastern Pacific coastlines, amply demonstrating the reliability of both concept and the hardware. It is not known whether Harrison heard of K1's success after James Cook's second voyage of discovery, but it is highly likely he would, as an old man, have been informed soon after Cook returned in July 1775. One certainly hopes so.

Left: Captain James Cook, by Nathaniel Dance, 1776. It was Cook's highly successful trials of K1 in his second and third voyages to the South Seas which proved to the world that Harrison's design was sound. [BHC2628]

Right: Watchmaker John Arnold by Mason Chamberlin, c.1765. It was Arnold alone who contributed the most, in detail, to the developed chronometer after Harrison.

Far right: Watchmaker Thomas Earnshaw, by Sir Martin Archer Shee, c.1808. Earnshaw's principal contribution was to standardise the form of the modern marine chronometer. [BHC2674]

Conclusion

The story of the marine chronometer, as such instruments became known, does not end here. Following Harrison's proof that such a timekeeper was possible, and with some of H4's essential design features published and available to watchmakers, a number of London makers found ways to simplify Harrison's design whilst preserving the fundamentals which ensured its good performance. It was not entirely in London that these design simplifications took place. The evidence suggests that one important concept, the 'free' or 'detached' escapement, central to modern chronometer design, was first thought of by the celebrated French pioneer Pierre Le Roy (1717–85).

Head and shoulders above the rest, among this 'next generation' of makers however, was John Arnold (1736–99). Encouraged by Nevil Maskelyne, who presented him with a copy of Harrison's *Principles* immediately after publication, Arnold was responsible for the majority of the design improvements in the modern marine chronometer. It then only remained for watchmaker Thomas Earnshaw (1749–1829) to standardize the form, which enabled the concept to be made quickly, cheaply, and in large numbers.

Thus, England remained at the forefront of chronometer and precision-watch production up to the end of the 19th century. It would not be an exaggeration to say that without Harrison's pioneering work, Britain's foreign trade would not have developed so extensively and its Empire could not have expanded as rapidly as it did. For nearly two centuries Britannia did indeed 'rule the waves', and Harrison, in no small measure, enabled it to do so.

Harrison's Legacy

Lieutenant-Commander Rupert T. Gould RN, photographed at his home in Epsom in 1924. He sits next to H3 and has one of the balances of H2 on his lap. [F4248]

*H*arrison's timekeepers themselves, however, suffered much less august fates. Ever since the disastrous trials under Maskelyne, the timekeepers remained at Greenwich. Save one impromptu cleaning session in the 1830s, they were virtually untouched until the 1920s. They lay in store, dirty, dismantled and decaying. It was only when Lieutenant-Commander Rupert T. Gould (1890–1948), a polymath and a keen amateur horologist, expressed an interest in them that they once again saw the light of day.

Gould described their condition: 'All were dirty, defective and corroded, while No.1, in particular, looked as though it had gone down with the *Royal George* and had been on the bottom ever since.' He continued: 'I could not bear to see them in this condition. It seemed to me such a futile, tragic ending to a great adventure. They were the first accurate marine timekeepers ever made – the life work of an original genius who was also an Englishman – and here they were, discarded … forgotten … buried. Surely they deserved a better fate.'

Gould wrote the definitive book on marine chronometers – a work so profoundly and thoroughly researched it still has no equal today – and was allowed to undertake their restoration. Initially he was only permitted to clean the corrosion off H1 (which was in by far the worst condition), but after successfully restoring its appearance (in 1920), Gould was allowed to restore H4 (1921), H2 (1923–25), the R.A.S. regulator (1927–29), H3 (1929–31) and then finally to complete a full restoration on H1 (1931–33).

A brilliant and remarkable polymath, Gould was fanatical in his interest in Harrison and was one of the 20th century's finest antiquarian horologists. So determined was he to see Harrison's legacy restored to its former glory, it not only took him much of the rest of his life, but caused him to lose nearly everything he held dear. This magnificent obsession of his ultimately contributed to the total breakdown of his marriage and the loss of his home, custody of his children, his closest friendships and even his job. He paid a very high price and it should be remembered that it is largely thanks to Gould's heroic efforts to save Harrison and his timekeepers from neglect, that we are able to enjoy seeing the timekeepers in their splendid, working condition to this day. It must also be said that, after Gould's death, the care of the timekeepers was undertaken by the Chronometer Section of the Ministry of Defence, who continued Gould's good works and improved one or two of his less elegant repairs.

So well was all this work carried out over previous years that today the large timekeepers run constantly, without fear of significant deterioration, and almost without breakdown. All that is required of their current custodians, the NMM's horological staff, is their daily winding, though there is still much to learn about their design and construction, and an ever-watchful eye is kept on their conservation to ensure they are preserved, with minimal change, for centuries to come.

Harrison Commemorated

*I*n recent years Harrison's fame has also undergone a renaissance. In 1993 the tercentenary of his birth was celebrated by the total refurbishment of the Royal Observatory's historic galleries, and the first edition of this book was produced on that occasion. The same year, Harrison medals were struck by the Royal Mint, the British Post Office released a celebratory set of Harrison stamps, and there was an important conference held at Harvard on the subject of Longitude. The conference resulted in the publication of the fine book *The Quest for Longitude*, but also inspired Dava Sobel to write her wonderful best-seller *Longitude* which brought Harrison's name to a much wider audience. Then there was the comedy show 'Only Fools and Horses' in 1996 (see p.66); and the new millennium in 2001 saw Harrison commemorated in a number of ways. 1993's tercentenary saw the start of petitions to have Harrison's great contribution recognized with a memorial in Westminster Abbey, finally bearing fruit in 2006 with a memorial tablet unveiled in the nave. Appropriately, this was right next to the grave of his old friend George Graham, who was buried in the same tomb as Thomas Thompion. With this memorial, and his own wonderful monuments in the form of the timekeepers preserved at Greenwich, we may rest assured that the name of John Harrison will be remembered and revered for centuries to come.

The memorial to John Harrison in Westminster Abbey, unveiled on 24 March 2006 by Prince Philip. Harrison's name is engraved across a bimetal, running due north–south across the tablet.

Suggested reading

R. T. Gould, *The Marine Chronometer*, Potter, London, 1923. Although over eighty years old, this is still the best book on marine chronometers.

H. Quill, *John Harrison*, Baker, London, 1966. Currently the only full biography of Harrison, and very well researched.

D. Sobel, *Longitude*, Walker, New York, 1995 and Penguin, London, 1996; new edition by Fourth Estate, London, 1998. The best-seller which tells the Harrison story in an exciting and accessible style.

W. Andrewes (ed.), *The Quest for Longitude*, Harvard, 1996. The proceedings of the Harvard Longitude conference of 1993, containing a series of erudite and definitive chapters on the history of longitude.

J. Betts, *Time Restored*, Oxford University Press/National Maritime Museum, 2006. The biography of R. T. Gould and the story of the Harrison timekeepers and their 20th-century restorations.

Photographic Acknowledgments

Illustrations (except where otherwise stated) are from the NMM collection and may be ordered by writing to the Picture Library, National Maritime Museum, Greenwich SE10 9NF, by fax to +44 (0)20 8312 6533 or email to picturelibrary@nmm.ac.uk. Please quote the image number provided alongside the relevant image caption. All images © copyright National Maritime Museum, London.

Illustrations are also reproduced by kind permission of the following:
Jonathan Betts, p.24, 58 (bottom left and right)
Andrew King, p.38
© copyright David Penney (www.antiquewatchstore.com), p.11, 12, 13, 17, 18, 37, 39, 40, 48, 49, 56, 57, 68
Dr John C. Taylor, p.36 (and also courtesy of the Earl of Yarborough), p.39 (left)
© copyright Trustees of the British Museum, p.91 (left)
© copyright Dean and Chapter of Westminster, p.95
© copyright National Archives, Kew, p.31
© copyright The Royal Collection 2007, Her Majesty Queen Elizabeth II, p.87
© copyright Sarah Stacey & Simon Stacey, p.93
Science Museum Pictorial/Science & Society Picture Library, cover, p.7, 28, 42
Worshipful Company of Clockmaker's/Bridgeman Art Library, p.29 (background), 35, 63, 64, 67, 75
Yale Center for British Art, Paul Mellon Collection, USA /The Bridgeman Art Library, p.88